How they get Rich?

by

Jack D. Chase

Table of Content

Synopsis

"All our dreams can come true, if we have the courage to pursue them" – Walt Disney

The world is changing, and the success stories from a decade ago are not relevant for the new generation today. Still, there are few success stories that the world has witnessed that will stay forever in our hearts and the ages to come as inspiration and motivation to make the world a better place through our ideas and the spark inside. I've written this book to humbly provide a tribute to those amazing people like Steve Jobs (May his soul rests in peace), Bill Gates, and others. Also, to help encourage the readers of the new and upcoming generation to pursue their dreams no matter how difficult they may seem initially.

Life is what you make of it, and that is the whole gist of the book. Willingness is the only factor that makes a difference between the successful and people who live with regrets.

Further, I dedicate this book to everyone who is out there trying to make it work for themselves and help their communities or impact on the global scale for betterment.

May Success be with You.

Jack D. Chase

Part 1:

That's how you play the game

Chapter 1 - Steve Jobs: From humble beginnings

The ones who are crazy enough to think they can change the world are the ones who do.

- Steve Jobs

Joanne Simpson and Abdulfattah John Jandali, two graduates of the University of Wisconsin, had a baby on Feb. 24, 1995, in San Francisco, California, and left their unnamed child for adoption. Job's father was a political science professor, and his mother worked as a speech therapist. His parents married soon after putting Jobs for adoption and had another child – Steve's biological sister, Mona Simpson. Jobs learned about their biological parents and parents when he turned 27. Clara and Paul Jobs adopted the unnamed infant and named him Steven Paul Jobs. Clara was an accountant, and Paul was a Coast Guard veteran and machinist. Jobs lived with his adoptive family in Mountain View in California, which later became Silicon Valley.

Young Jobs used to work on electronics with his father in the family garage, and that's what instilled confidence in him at an early age.

Being highly intelligent and an out-of-the-box thinker, Jobs had trouble going through the conventional schooling at Homestead High School and struggled throughout his educational journey. Jobs turned into a prankster in elementary school due to boredom, and his school teacher used to bribe him to study.

After a difficult time in school, he enrolled at Reed College in Portland, Oregon. Although he was intelligent, he lacked direction and dropped out of college after the first six months and got into 18 months to a creative class at school where he learned about calligraphy. That developed his passion for typography.

Jobs met his co-founding partner - Steve Wozniak, when he was studying at Homestead High School. Wozniak was attending the University of California, Berkeley at that time. They both shared the love of electronics, and back then, not many people knew about the chips' functionality and capabilities. Both shared an independent attitude about things in the world, but a strong bond for engineering kept them together and, at the same time, respected the differences between the two.

In 1976, Jobs and Wozniak started Apple Computer out of Jobs' family garage. He bought initial funding from Jobs, who sold his Volkswagen bus, and Wozniak, who sold his scientific calculator. What started from a garage positively transformed the computer industry by making them smaller, cheaper and accessible technology for a low-level consumer.

In 1979 Steve Jobs led several Apple engineers to Xerox Corporation's Palo Alto Research Center (PARC) to experience the revolutionary graphical user interface under PARC development. Subsequently, Jobs left the engineering division to head a smaller group working on a lower-cost model of the Macintosh. Both Apple computers were redesigned using the PARC ideas, but Steve Jobs favored the Mac, or Mac, as the new computer. Jobs valued his engineers and treated them as artists, but he was also uncompromising and asked for a redesign of an internal circuit board simply because he thought it was not sophisticated enough. He was renowned for his insistence that the Macintosh not merely be great but "insanely great."

Wozniak was in charge of making the technology more user-friendly, and Jobs was focused on Marketing that technology. The first price tag for Apple computers was $666.66 each – which was for Apple I, and it earned the company more than $750,000. Three years later, with Apple II, its sales increased by seven hundred percent to $139m.

Only four years after the launch, Apple Computer became a publicly-traded company with a market value of $1.2b after the first day of trading. Jobs inducted a marketing genius John Sculley from Pepsi-Cola to take over the CEO role for Apple.

Few products after Apple II has design and functionality flaws which caused a setback for Apple, and that made room for IBM to step ahead and lead the sales over Apple.

In January 1984, Jobs introduced the Macintosh in a brilliantly choreographed demonstration that was the centerpiece of an extraordinary publicity campaign. It would later be referred to as the "toothed comb" of marketing.

Apple released the first version of the Macintosh Operating System (OS), marketing the computer as a lifestyle that depicts the user's romantic, youthful and creative nature. Although the sales and performance were superior to IBM, the new OS was not compatible with IBM hardware.

Sculley, who was brought in by Jobs himself, started doubting Jobs and considered him a negative impact on the company. Since Jobs didn't have an official title in the company, Sculley and other board members pushed him to a marginalized position, making Jobs leave Apple in 1985 after selling all his shares in the company.

Initial Macs were underpowered and expensive, which resulted in disappointing sales for all Mac products. Apple steadily improved their computer, leading to it being a staple and direct influence for all future computer interfaces. Jobs' apparent unwillingness to correct the trend led to tensions in the company, and in 1985 Apple's board of directors removed him as CEO.

In 1985, after exiting from Apple, Jobs started a new hardware and software company called NeXT, Inc. The company struggled through its attempt to sell the specialized OS in America. After 11 years of operations, the company was acquired by Apple in 1996.

A year after launching NeXT, Jobs purchased an animation company from George Lucas, which later became Pixar Animation Studios. Jobs injected his own money into the company, which was about $50m, showed how much he believed in the company.

In late 1996, Apple, under dire financial straits and near bankruptcy, hired a new CEO, Dr. Gilbert Amelio. When Amelio learned that the company, with intense research efforts, had not developed an acceptable replacement for the Macintosh's aging operating system, he bought Jobs' company for more than $400 million—and brought Jobs back to Apple on a consultant role. However, Apple's board of directors soon got disappointed with the Amelio's inability to turn the finances around. In June 1997, they requested Apple's prodigal co-founder to lead the company once again. Jobs quickly forged a strategic alliance with Apple's former enemy, Microsoft, broke up Amelio's Mac-clone agreements, and sped up Apple's product line. He also designed an award-winning set of ad campaigns urging people to buy Apple products. Apple also resisted the temptation to create machines that ran Microsoft's Windows OS, and he did not, as others urged, spin-off Apple as a software-only company. Companies believed Apple would be the only major personal computer maker to devise a unique operating system platform.

In 1997, Jobs was brought back to Apple to his CEO, and again he revived the Apple brand as he did back in the 1970s. With a new management team at his disposal, he took the stock options and a self-imposed annual salary of $1/year – Jobs launched all amazing products like iMac through effective branding campaigns that caught the consumers' attention once again.

Innovate he did! In 1998, Jobs introduced the iMac, a complex egg-shaped computer that offered the high-speed processing necessary for a new generation of sophisticated applications. (The Macintosh computer went on to become the nation's top-selling personal computer, and Steve Jobs was able to announce consistent profits for the once-moribund company.) The next year, he triumphantly returned with the classy iBook, a laptop computer built for students, and the G4, a desktop computer sufficiently powerful that (Apple boasted) it could not be exported into certain foreign countries because it qualified as a supercomputer. Though Apple did not regain its industry dominance at the time, Steve Jobs had saved his company, and in the process, had re-established himself as a master marketer and visionary.

In 2007, Apple's quarterly reports highly improved, and stock prices went up to $199.99/share – which was a record-breaking number at that time. The company's profits went up to a staggering $1.58b with $18b in the banks with zero debt.

In 2011, Forbes estimated Jobs' net worth at around $6-7b, acquired from the sale of Pixar to the Disney Corporation in 2006. If Jobs had not sold his Apple shares in 1985, he would have been worth $36 billion when he left the company he founded and helmed for over a decade.

Jobs was one of the first entrepreneurs to understand that a computer would appeal to a broad audience, and in fact, could be marketed to a younger demographic. In light of Jobs's suggestion, Wozniak designed a superior model, the Apple II, as well as a plastic case to encase the unit.

Jobs managed to obtain funding, distribution, and publicity for Apple Computer, Inc. on the same year that the Apple II was completed. The machine did well, helping to shape the computer industry.

In 2007 Jobs introduced the touch-screen iPhone, a mobile telephone with capabilities to play MP3s and videos and access the Internet. Later that year, Apple introduced the iPod Touch, which included Wi-Fi capabilities, an iPhone-like touch screen, and gaming capabilities. With the iTunes Store's use to sell Apple and third-party software, the iPhone and iPod Touch soon boasted more games than any other portable gaming system. Jobs pointed out that iPhone and iPod Touch games would be improved over time. In an interesting development, as Apple did not support game developers in its early years out of fear of its computers not being taken seriously as business machines, it had now accepted a greater role in the gaming business to go along with its move into telecommunications.

On Aug. 2, 2018, Apple became the first publicly-traded company worth $1T, and Microsoft joined the club on Apr. 30, 2019, becoming the world's most valuable company. On Jan. 16, 2020, Alphabet became a $1 trillion corporation, followed by Amazon on Feb. 4.

Each of these companies' market value has fluctuated, and maintaining a valuation of $1 trillion within a volatile market can be tough to do. However, the iPhone has become the world's most popular phone has much to do with the legacy and accomplishments of Steve Jobs.

Steve Jobs passed away on Oct. 5, 2011, at 56 years and two months, following his second departure from Apple Inc. for the second time. Jobs was a true entrepreneur, and his rise to fame is Apple's story as a company.

Steve Jobs and Steve Wozniak founded Apple in 1977, and the first Apple that they released was the Apple I and Apple II, respectively.

The Summary

- Apple was taken public by Jobs and Wozniak in 1980, with Jobs the visionary and Wozniak the innovative genius.
- Executive John Scully began working for Apple in 1983 and was promoted to CEO in 1985.
- Upon his move away from Apple, Jobs invested in animation producer Pixar and founded NeXT, leading him to Apple.
- Jobs returned to Apple in the late 1990s and spent the years until his death in 2011 revamping the company, introducing the iPod, iPhone, and iPad, transforming technology and communication in the process.

It's easy to define the Job's success over the tie, but it takes dedication and passion for walking the other way, and among hundreds of possible lessons, there are a few lessons that stick out. First, innovation is essential to success, but innovation requires one to be mindful of marketing. Second, there are no paths that consistently lead to success. Jobs would be a footnote today if he did not return to Apple in the late 80s 1990s. Jobs was once fired from the company he founded due to his poor leadership. Instead of changing, he bided his time, eventually seizing and maintaining leadership again for the third time.

There are many lessons to be learned from Steve Jobs' life, just like from many entrepreneurs' lives. The sheer hubris of the entrepreneurial spirit, the idea that someone can do something bigger and better than it has been done before, always bears watching and studying, whether to imitate or to marvel at what this highly driven confidence can create.

Chapter 2 – Jeff Bezos: Mind your own business

Jeff Bezos was born on Jan. 12, 1964, in Seattle, Washington. Bezos was born to a teenage mother and a 21-year-old biological father. He is an American entrepreneur who has played a key role in the growth of e-commerce as the founder and CEO of Amazon.com, Inc. - an online platform of books initially and later offered a wide variety of products. Through his guidance, Amazon.com became the world's largest online retailer and the model for online sales.

The founder of the Amazon e-commerce company, Jeff Bezos, is the Washington Post owner and a space exploration company, Blue Origin. His extensive business holdings have made him extremely wealthy in the international market. Bezos began his university education at Princeton University with a focus in computer science and electrical engineering. After completing his degree, he worked on Wall Street as a senior vice president at

D.E. Shaw. After four years, Bezos quit his lucrative employment as a vice president at D. E. Shaw to open the online bookstore Amazon.com.

Bezos was interested in how things work from a very young age, so he set up experiments in his parents' garage and rigged electrical contraptions around his house as a child.

He moved to Miami as a teenager, where he developed a love for science and high-tech gadgets. He started The Dream Institute, an educational summer camp for fourth through sixth-grade kids – TDI was his first business.

Bezos went on to work at several different firms, including Fitel, Bankers Trust, and subsequently Amazon. In 1990, Bezos became the D.E. Shaw's newest junior vice president.

Despite his lucrative career as a finance professional, Bezos was courageous enough to enter the developing world of internet commerce. He left his job in 1994 and moved to Seattle to take advantage of the online market's untapped potential.

Bezos opened Amazon in July 1994 after he asked 300 friends and family to test his new site. A few Amazon employees began developing software with Bezos in his garage, which later transitioned into a two-bedroom house equipped with three Sun Micro stations.

The company's initial success was meteoric. With no marketing measures, Amazon.com sold books across the United States and abroad within thirty days. Sales grew at an exponentially higher rate in two months, which was more than what Bezos and his startup team had anticipated.

When Amazon.com went public in 1997, many market analysts questioned whether they could survive in an increasingly competitive marketplace. Two years later, the startup outperformed competitors and then went on to become the largest e-commerce player.

Bezos continued to diversify Amazon's offerings in 1998 by selling CDs and other products and later started clothing lines, electronics, and toys.

Although many .coms of the '90s failed within a decade, Amazon boomed with sales that were over $17 billion in 2011.

As part of Jeff Bezos' 2018 shareholder letter, Amazon announced it had surpassed 100 million subscribers to its Prime

Video subscription service. As of September 2018, Amazon was worth more than $1T. The company surpassed Facebook as the most valuable company in the world.

Amazon recently announced that it would be raising the minimum wage of its workers to $15 per hour. The company is still criticized for poor working conditions and the fast-paced work environment, with employees protesting on Prime Day.

In 2013, on Aug. 5, Bezos bought The Washington Post and other affiliated publications with The Washington Post Co. for $250 million.

The deal marked the end of the four-generation reign of The Post Co. by the Graham family. Donald E. Graham is the chairman of the company, and his niece, Katharine Graham, is the publisher.

In 2000, Bezos founded Blue Origin LLC, a space exploration company that seeks to make space travel more affordable. For several years, the company operated without much notice.

In 2016, Bezos hosted reporters at Amazon headquarters in Kent, Washington, to showcase its cutting-edge technology. He believes that humans will not only visit but eventually settle on other planets. Since 2017, Jeff Bezos has committed $1b in stocks set to go into Blue Origin.

Half a year later, he revealed the Blue Origin lunar lander showing that the company is conducting test flights of its suborbital New Shepard rocket.

In August 2020, NASA announced that Blue Origin was one of 13 companies selected to collaborate on 19 different technology projects to reach the moon and Mars. Blue Origin focused on landing humans safely on the moon and developing special nozzles for rockets with liquid-fueled engines. The company is also working with NASA to create a seaplane reused on future rocket launches.

In 2018, Bezos launched the Bezos Day One Fund, which focuses on "funding existing nonprofits that help homeless families, and creating a network of new, nonprofit tier-one preschools in low-income communities." The announcement came a year after Bezos had asked his Twitter followers how to donate part of his fortune. Bezos established the organization with MacKenzie before their divorce, and he transferred $2 billion to fund the nonprofit. As the richest man in the world, Bezos had previously been criticized for his lack of charitable donations.

On Jan. 30, 2018, Amazon, Berkshire Hathaway, and JPMorgan Chase created a new healthcare company to provide healthcare for their employees in the US.

The release says the healthcare company will be freed from the profit-making incentives and constraints that might hinder their ability to lower costs and improve the patient experience.

In mid-2020, Amazon announced that CEO Jeff Bezos would be stepping down from his corporate board role. He will, after an executive chair, join Amazon's board of directors.

The Summary

Jeff Bezos, byname of Jeffrey Preston Bezos, American executive who has been a major force in the growth of e-commerce as the founder and chief executive officer of Amazon.com, Inc., an online merchant of books and later of a wide variety of products. Through his guidance, Amazon.com became the world's largest online retailer and the model for online sales.

"What we need to do is always lean into the future; when the world changes around you and when it changes against you – what used to be a tail wind is now a head wind – you have to lean into that and figure out what to do because complaining isn't a strategy." – Jeff Bezos

"The common question that gets asked in business is, 'why?' That's a good question, but an equally valid question is, 'why not?'" – Jeff bezos

Chapter 3 –
Bill Gates: Step up

"As we look ahead into the next century, leaders will be those who empower others." - Bill Gates

Gates was born in 1955 as William Henry Gates III, in Seattle, Washington. Gates grew up in a well-off family with his two older sisters. The father, William H. Gates Sr., was an up-and-coming law-school graduate when he met his future wife, Mary. She was an athletic, extroverted and outgoing student at the University of Washington.

The Gates family was warm and accepting, and the three children were encouraged towards excellence. Gates showed early competitive signs in his parental involvement with extracurricular events at their summer home on Puget Sound. He enjoyed playing board games, such as Risk and quickly learned how to play Monopoly.

Gates had a very close relationship with his mother, who devoted her time to working on civic affairs and helping lead charities after a brief career as a teacher. She was a member of several corporate boards, including those of the International Business Machines Corporation and the Seattle First Interstate Bank (IBM). She would frequently take Gates to community meetings and educational institutions.

Gates read a lot when he was young, including many reference books like encyclopedias. At the age of 11 or 12, Gates's parents noticed that Gates's behavior had changed. He was doing well in school, but he sometimes avoided social interaction, and his parents were concerned that he might avoid social interaction in the future.

Though Gates and his family were dedicated believers in public education, when Gates was 13, he was transferred to Lakeside, a private school in Seattle. Throughout his school career, he excelled in math, science, English, and drama.

During the school year, a Seattle computer company donated technology to Lakeside School. Gates became fascinated by a computer's possibilities and spent much of his time devoted to his computer. He was the creator of a computer program that allowed users to play tic-tac-toe against the machine.

Gates joined Lakeview in 1973. He scored a perfect 1600 on the college SAT, a feat he boasted about for several years after his admission to the school he eventually attended.

Gates was accepted into Harvard University in the fall of 1973, as he originally had intentions of pursuing a career in law. While his parents were disappointed, Gates pursued a prosperous business by creating Microsoft with his partner, Allen.

Gates spent the majority of class time in the computer lab. He did not have a study regimen and instead got by on a few hours of sleep and used to pass the tests with just a decent grade.

In 1975, Bill Gates and Paul Allen founded Microsoft, a combination of the words "micro-computer" and "software." The company's first product was a programming language called BASIC, which ran on early microcomputers.

At first, things weren't altogether smooth sailing. Even though Microsoft didn't make much money off their BASIC computer language, it wasn't doing much for their overhead. According to Gates' later recollection, less than 10% of the people who purchased BASIC spent any money on the software.

Microsoft's BASIC software was quite popular with computer hobbyists, who received early versions and passed them around, copying and distributing them for free. Until the early 1980s, many personal computer enthusiasts had no financial interest in the industry, while Gates felt otherwise. He considered free distribution of software as a form of theft, especially when it is helping in selling products.

In 1976, Gates wrote an open letter to computer hobbyists, stating that continued distribution and use of the software without paying for it would discourage the author from spending time and effort into writing quality code. The letter was unpopular with computer enthusiasts, but Bill Gates was unwilling to compromise his beliefs and would frequently use the claim of innovation against critics.

Gates clashed with the president of MITS, Ed Roberts, resulting in frequent disagreements. Gates was at odds with Roberts over software development and the direction of the company. Roberts considered Gates wealthy and spoiled.

After leaving MITS in 1977, Roberts returned to Georgia, went back to medical school, and became a doctor.

Gates and Allen worked alone. The company sued the new MITS owner to retained the rights to develop, market, and distribute the software they had created. Microsoft developed software in different formats for other companies, and in 1979, Gates moved the company's operations to Bellevue, Washington.

Gates became eager to return to the Pacific Northwest and continued working hard. All 25 employees of the young, up-and-coming company had various responsibilities ranging from product development to company growth to market penetration.

Despite starting on shaky footing, in 1979, Microsoft was in the $2.5 million range. At the age of 23, Gates took a leadership role within Microsoft. With his software development and sales skills, he led the company and gave a public face to its business. Gates reviewed every line of code shipped by Microsoft, more so than any other Microsoft software engineer.

Despite the intensely competitive rivalry, Microsoft and Apple had much of their early innovations in common. In 1981, with Steve Jobs at the helm, Apple invited Microsoft to join as a partner to develop software for Apple Mac computers. Developers began working on Microsoft applications while concurrently working on software for the Macintosh. Some shared names can be seen in the Microsoft and Macintosh operating systems.

This knowledge led to the development of Windows, a system that uses a mouse to drive a graphical interface, displaying text and images on a screen. Contrasting with the previous MS-DOS system where all text formatting was displayed on the screen as code and not how it would be displayed.

Gates recognized the significance of the threat that this kind of software posed to MS-DOS and Microsoft as a whole. The competing VisiCorp software's graphic imagery would be much easier to comprehend and use than a text-based program for the buyer who has everyday usage.

Gates offered a new campaign that an upcoming Microsoft operating system would incorporate a graphical user interface. It was called "Windows," which would be compatible with all program and operating system products based on the Microsoft OS.

As an innovative marketing tactic, it was brilliant. Over 30% of the computer market used the MS-DOS system and begrudgingly waiting for Windows OS release. Without the computer users' willingness to change formats, software developers were unwilling to write programs for the VisiCorp system, and ultimately the product lost momentum by early 1985.

Despite Microsoft's success, Gates never felt completely secure. Gates was always checking on the competition, which resulted in innovation and competitiveness in his work. Gates' secretary reported that one day at work, "someone was sleeping under her desk. She considered calling security but eventually decided against it since it was Bill."

Gates' intelligence allowed him to see various software industry sides, including product development, corporate strategy, and business development. When analyzing any corporate move, he considered all possible causes and then considered how to respond if any of those cases happened.

He was surprised that the others did not share his dedication. He was known for his aggressive management style, which made employees feel they had to be creative and perform well. An unprepared presenter could receive a scathing remark from Bill Gates.

It was as much a test of whether the employee was the best at the Job as it was Bill Gates' passion for his company. He was constantly adjusting to make sure that his ideas were not being challenged.

Outside the company, Gates became known as a highly competitive rival. Several technology companies began to develop an alternative to Microsoft Windows in response to OS/2. In response to the pressure, Gates put more focus on Windows and improved its operation and usefulness.

In March 1986, Gates released Microsoft to the public for $21.00 a share, making him an instant millionaire. Bill Gates held 45% of the company's total share value.

Eventually, the company's stock increased in value and had many splits, giving it various valuations. In 2000, Gates became a billionaire as shares surpassed $90.75. Since then, Gates has remained near the top of Forbes' list of the 400 Richest Americans. With stock prices at an all-time high and Gates' wealth reaching new heights, his net worth soon topped the $100 billion mark.

In 1987, a 23-year-old Microsoft product manager named Melinda French caught Bill Gates's attention (then 32 years old). Melinda, with her charisma, was an ideal match for Gates. Eventually, their relationship grew as they discovered an intimate and intellectual connection, and in 1994, Melinda and Bill got married in Hawaii.

In 1989, Microsoft introduced the Microsoft Office suite that included a Word processor, spreadsheet, and database programs compatible with Microsoft products.

Throughout the 1990s, the American government sued Microsoft over its business practices, all handled by Bill Gates and his team on fair terms. They were all sure throughout that they were not involved in any illegal business practice.

In 2000, Bill Gates stepped down as Chief Executive Officer of Microsoft and turned over the Job to a longtime business associate, Steve Ballmer. As the chief software architect, Gates positioned himself to focus more intensely on the business applications software, though he remained the board's chairman.

In 2006, Bill Gates announced that he intended to dedicate more time to the Bill & Melinda Gates Foundation. His last day at Microsoft was Jun. 27, 2008.

In February 2014, Gates stepped down as chairman of Microsoft Corporation to assume a new position at the technology consulting firm Hogan Lovells. 46-years old, Satya Nadella replaced Bill Gates.

Bill Gate's success story is driven by resilience, genius, and dedication to innovate to make lives better through technology and humanity.

Part 2:

Where you belong?

Chapter 4 –

Ralph Lauren: 'Millionaire' is my future goal

"I am not looking like Armani today and somebody else tomorrow," says designer Ralph Lauren. "I look like Ralph Lauren. And my goal is to constantly move in fashion and move in style without giving up what I am." – Ralph Lauren

And since he launched his fashion label, Polo, in 1967, he's done just that.

Ralph Lauren's first job in fashion was as a clerk in a menswear department in a men's clothing store. The brand he created, Polo, is now one part of an international luxury fashion conglomerate that includes fragrances, home furnishings, and dining. Lauren, a major sponsor of cancer research, has also made a fortune in ranches and a huge collection of rare and classic cars.

He was born in the Bronx, New York City. His birth name is Ralph Lifshitz, and he was the third of four siblings. He was a child of Ashkenazi Jewish immigrants who fled Belarus, and he grew up in the Mosholu Parkway area of Brooklyn.

On his 16th birthday, Ralph decided to change his name to Lauren to receive respect at school. Being the eldest son, Lenny took the family surname. Ralph was known for his distinctive fashion sense as a teen, finding inspiration in screen icons like Fred Astaire and Cary Grant while having a taste for classic preppy wear and vintage looks. He continued his college education at Baruch College, where he studied business for two years. After growing tired of the military, Lauren decided to work at Brooks Brothers.

In 1967, Lauren launched a line of men's neckties with a more masculine fit, which he branded as "Polo" and sold through department stores. Lauren received a $30,000 loan that allowed him to design his business, eventually expanding his designs that included an entire men's line.

In 1970, Lauren was named the Coty Award Winner for his winning men's designs. After receiving recognition, he subsequently released a line of women's tailored suits. In 1972, Lauren Liddell released a short-sleeved cotton shirt in 24 different colors. This design featured the company's namesake, and a member of the French polo team was a key factor in the brand's success.

In the 1970s, Lauren made a foray into the film business by designing costumes for the 1974 film adaptation of The Great Gatsby, starring Robert Redford and Mia Farrow. Lauren has credits for helping cast members of 1975's The Wild Party, including James Coco and Raquel Welch. After designing the distinctive look of stars like Diane Keaton in the 1977 comedy Annie Hall, the designer became well known.

Sometime in the future, Lauren was drawn to a television program that embodies his particular style, Downton Abbey. Later, he created the show's fall collection and sponsored its last season.

Lauren gained popularity by capitalizing on aspirational style elements and key symbols of the upper-class British gentry while also referencing the American upper class's aesthetics. Some have criticized his fashion choices for not being particularly innovative and being perceived as appealing and popular by many consumers. Lauren later broadened his company's reach by creating a clothing line known as Ralph Lauren Purple, a line of furniture known as Ralph Lauren Home, and a line of fragrances known as Ralph Lauren. Polo currently produces clothing for men, women, and children and sells in hundreds of different countries worldwide.

In 1983 Lauren released his first home collection, and in 1986, Polo Ralph Lauren opened his first store on Madison Avenue at 72nd Street in his hometown of Rhinelander.

In 1997, Ralph Lauren received a CFDA Outstanding Achievement Award, and later, Ralph Lauren Media was founded in the year 2000. In 2004, a lifestyle line of Rugby was introduced targeted at younger demographics. In 2007, Lauren received the first American Fashion Legend Award, and two products were added to Polo Ralph Lauren: watches and jewelry.

Polo rapidly expanded in the 1980s and 1990s, and clothing boutiques spread across the country and overseas. In 1986, Lauren opened his company's flagship store in New York, which now has stores on Madison & Grand. After Goldman Sachs purchased the majority of Polo Ralph Lauren in the mid-1990s, Polo Ralph Lauren went public in Jun. 11, 1997. Lauren's success in marketing Polo has earned Lauren a fortune estimated at more than six billion dollars, making Lauren one of the 200 richest people in the world.

After a year of falling stock prices, Lauren stepped down as CEO and appointed Larsson, the Old Navy's global president, to take over as CEO. Lauren took on the role of chairman of his company's board of directors and chief creative officer.

The firm started making women's clothing bearing the Ralph Lauren name in 1997, and after the IPO, the company went public. Ralph, the first designer to reap the financial riches of his own branded store.

Lauren had also designed clothes for the USA Olympic team, though controversy ensued when it was revealed that the uniforms for the 2012 summer games were made in China.

Ralph's story defines a man of vision, who understood fashion and delivered innovation to clothing, and his vision spread across the globe and is loved everywhere equally.

> *"The clothes that I design and everything I've done is about how people live and how they want to live and how they dream they'll live. That's what I do."*

"My life has been a dream. If someone had to write a story about it, it would seem a little unreal. It's the kind of story I would read and say, Nah, that's not possible." – Ralph Lauren

Chapter 5 –

Do Won Chang: Make it big

Do Won Chang, known by the name Don, is the founder of Forever 21 – a hot selling store initiated in the United States of America and has branches around the globe and generates billions in sales every year. He started the store with his wife – and both worth $6.3m, listed among the top businessperson's list at #248.

He is a millionaire today, but he has had a wrecked beginning, which keeps him humbled going through life. He spends a big chunk of his money and time on multiple causes close to his heart.

Do Won Chang was born in 1954 in a small village in Seoul, South Korea, called Myeong-Dong. He always had an amazing work ethic – he worked in coffee shops and started his coffee delivery service.

In 1981, Don moved to America with his wife, Jin Sook. While struggling his way through life in America, he at one point had three different jobs, a servant at a coffee shop, a janitor, and a gas station attendant.

He noticed that all the wealthy people around him worked in fashion, which made him realize that his ticket to success is through the fashion industry, and well, wasn't he right?

In 1984, through the collections of wages from the three jobs, Don opened his first store in LA's Highland Park area. He named it Fashion 21 and targeted his fellow Korean-Americans. Within a year, sales soared from $35k to $700k.

To appeal to more customers, he changed the store's name to Forever 21, and that surely worked as he was able to open eleven more stores within the next five years in the United States and even in his hometown, Myeong-Dong, South Korea.

In 2009 when the US recession hit, it made one of a tough year in American history for everyone, including the businesses. The recession forced Don to close seven of his stores, but his dedication and motivation towards success didn't let him stay on the business roadside. Forever 21 soon recovered and continued to grow through high ceilings, and today it has more than 600 stores around the world, including one in London and one in Birmingham, UK.

Don is a man of faith and comes from a family of committed Christians. Jin Sook went to the top of a mountain to pray, and Chang mentions Bible as his favorite book. Both have two daughters together, Linda – who is the marketing manager of Forever 21, and the second one is Esther, who heads up the merchandising. Despite being a global brand, it is still a family-owned business and has not been floated in the stock market yet. Jin Sook is the buyer of Fashion 21 and personally reviews four hundred designs each day.

Chapter 6 –

Howard Schultz: From the depths of uncertainty

Howard Schultz was born on Jul. 19, 1953, in Brooklyn, New York. He graduated from Northern Michigan University in Communications. By the mid of his career working in the coffee industry – he established a company through which he acquired Starbucks with the backing of investors and took over Starbucks as CEO and chairman in 1987. Schultz announced in 2000 that he would leave Starbucks' CEO position. He went on to be reinstated to lead the company in 2008. He then announced his presidential run in 2020 before ending his campaign in September of that year.

After his birth in Brooklyn, New York, he moved to the Bayview Housing Projects in Brooklyn, New York, with his family when he was three years old. Schultz was a natural athlete, which made him excel in basketball and football, which further complimented his physical fitness. He received a full scholarship to Northern Michigan University in the 1970s.

After finishing his Bachelor of Science in communication in 1975, Schultz found work for Hammarplast as an appliance salesman to sell European coffee makers in the United States. As a regional sales manager in the early 1980s, Schultz noticed that he was selling more coffee machines to a small business in Seattle, WA called Starbucks Coffee and Tea Company than to Macy's. "Every month, every quarter, these numbers were going up, even though Starbucks just had a few stores," Schultz recalled. "And I said, 'I gotta go up to Seattle.'"

Howard Schultz can still remember the first time he entered the original Starbucks store, which opened in 1971. At that time, Starbucks had only been around for only ten years and had not been expanded to other locations. Starbucks founder Jerry Baldwin and his college buddies Gordon Bowker and Zev Siegl founded the company. The three friends created the logo for their own coffee company.

“When I walked in this store for the first time,” he said, “I knew I was home. I can’t say for sure. But I knew I was at a unique place globally, and the product fit my personality. I had never had a cup of coffee that tasted that good. I met the founders of the company and learned that coffee tastes great because of the company’s commitment to quality.” Schultz had no idea how truly beneficial his introduction to the company was or how pivotal his role became in creating the modern Starbucks.

In 1982, Howard Schultz was hired as director of retail operations and marketing for Starbucks. His impression of Howard at that time was that he was an excellent communicator. “One to one, he still is.”

Early on, Schultz established a corporate culture within Starbucks by making the company’s mission his own. When traveling in Milan, Italy, he noticed that many restaurants serve coffee. Then it occurred to him: Starbucks should also offer drinks besides coffee. “I remember something. Not only the romance of coffee, but the sense of community nature provides. And the connection that people had to coffee—the people and the place, “ Schultz recalled. “And after a week in Italy, I was so convinced with such unbridled enthusiasm that I couldn’t wait to get back to Seattle to talk about the fact that I had seen the future.”

Schultz's zealous efforts to open coffee bars at Starbucks locations were at odds with Starbucks' founders. "We said, 'Oh no, that's not for us,'" Siegl recalled. "Since the '70s, we have served coffee in our store. We even had a fully-functional espresso machine inside the workplace. Although, we were involved in a bean business." Regardless, Schultz was determined until the owners finally let him open an espresso bar in a new location. It was an instant success, attracting hundreds of people each day, introducing a new language, coffeehouses' language, to Seattle in 1984.

The success of the coffee bar demonstrated to the founders and agreed with Schultz's vision for Starbucks' future. They didn't want to grow too large. Schultz left Starbucks in 1985 and started his chain of coffee shops that was successful.

Two years later, Schultz purchased Starbucks, merging Il Giornale with Starbucks. Next, he became the CEO and chairman of Starbucks (known after that as the Starbucks Coffee Company). Schultz had to convince his investors that Americans would pay top dollar for a beverage that they were accustomed to receiving for just a few pennies. At that time, most Americans had no idea of where good coffee beans came from.

In 2000, Schultz publicly announced his departure as CEO. Only after eight years, however, did he return to head the company. In a 2009 interview with CBS, Schultz stated, "We're not in the business of filling bellies; we're in the business of filling souls."

In 2006, Howard Schultz was ranked No. 359 on Forbes's "Forbes 400" list, America's richest and most powerful people. In 2013, he was ranked No. 311 on the Forbes list of billionaires around the globe.

There is no one company selling more coffee drinks to people than Starbucks. By 2012, Starbucks had expanded to encompass approximately 17,600 locations in 39 markets worldwide, and the company's market cap was valued at approximately $35.6 billion. By 2014, Starbucks' worldwide presence was 21,000+, with a market cap of $60 billion. The popular coffee company reportedly opens two or three new retail locations each day and attracts around 60 million people each week. The company's website asserts that they are dedicated to sourcing and roasting only the highest-quality arabica coffee.

On Jun. 4, 2018, Starbucks released a press release announcing that Schultz would step down as chairman, and the position of chairman emeritus was announced. Myron Ullman was appointed as the chairman, and Mellody Hobson's position was appointed for the associate vice-chairman's role.

Schultz left Starbucks to spend more time at home and work on a book about Starbucks' social impact efforts.

In an interview on Jul. 9, 2018, Starbucks CEO Howard Schultz addressed investor concerns that Starbucks is experiencing a slowdown in China. He also discussed a possible collaboration with Alibaba Group Holding Ltd.'s (BABA) billionaire founder Jack Ma, which became a reality later that year. Starbucks and Alibaba announced a different deal to work together to create an order and delivery system for consumers in China.

Schultz declared his plans to run for president in January of 2020 as an independent candidate. However, in September 2019, he concluded his campaign for the year and probably won't run for the position again.

Howard Schultz's story portrays a dreamer and a resilient person who knew what to do and how to do it. The clarity and vision are required to make a dream come true – at the end of the day, these two things help understand your purpose in life. Schultz is a perfect example for people who wish to pursue dreams in life, and his ability to take the right steps can be considered a benchmark for the people who are willing to follow the same trail he once followed.

Summary:

- Howard Schultz took over Starbucks and made the company into one of the world's top coffee brands.
- Schultz expanded Starbucks from 11 stores to more than 30,000 stores worldwide and created a unique social hangout place for people with his friendly service.
- In 2018, Schultz departed from his executive position at the company he joined nearly 30 years ago.
- Schultz sought a 2020 presidential bid but later clarified that he would not run, stating that running would risk Donald Trump's re-election.

"When you're surrounded by people who share a passionate commitment around a common purpose, anything is possible."

Dream more than others think practical. Expect more than others think possible. Care more than others thinks wise.

Howard Schultz

Part 3:

It's never too late

Chapter 7 –

It's all about the mindset

A mindset is the sum of your feelings, opinions, beliefs, and thoughts that help you see the world. Think of your mind as a filtering device that narrows what you perceive.

Our education, upbringing, religion, and experience help to shape our thoughts and beliefs. Our mind is in a fixed state rather than flexible and fluid. Therefore, determines how you perceive and react to specific environmental factors.

"There are no limitations to the mind except those we admit," Napoleon Hill said. The idea that poverty and riches stem from thought.

We are all constantly shifting on a spectrum of two different mindsets or ways of thinking, 1. a fixed or 2. a growth mindset, as explained by Stanford University psychologist Carol Dweck in her book 'Mindset: The New Psychology of Success. The mindsets of self-determination and efficacy ultimately impact the degree to which we feel comfortable pushing ourselves to develop a specific skill or how proactive we are about a challenging task.

If you have a fixed mindset, you believe we're either born with particular skills or don't have them at all, and there's not much anyone can do to change that. People with a fixed mindset tend to avoid challenges, give up easily when they face one, ignore or dismiss constructive feedback, and sometimes feel threatened by others or new situations. This mindset negatively impacts their propensity to learn. Maybe a belief that they always have to appear intelligent to be valued and successful. As a result, they are less likely to push themselves out of their comfort zones and learn new things along the way for fear that they will be humiliated or make a mistake.

By contrast, those with a growth mindset believe that abilities and skills can always be improved by effort and practice. They believe that their capacity to learn and their capacity to grow within their intellectual capacity can be developed. They persevere even during stressful times, often taking on board and even utilizing feedback and ideas from those around them. They tend to see life as a never-ending opportunity to figure out new things and appreciate that failure is an essential component of learning and progression. They recognize that mastery of a skill requires dedication, practice, and a long-term commitment.

It is equally important to understand what a growth mindset is not. The concept is not about suggesting anyone could do anything. Nor is it an argument that everyone should possess a given passion or capability. It is acknowledging that, for the most part, we can all improve our capabilities in a wide range of areas, areas we never thought we would be able to get better at if we adopt the right mindset, practice, and don't give up.

It's also worth adding at this point that the research indicates that there's simply no such thing as one person with a fixed mindset and another with a growth mindset. It's just not as clear-cut as mentioned earlier. As mentioned earlier, we're all on a spectrum between the two, to a lesser or greater extent, often switching from one to the other in certain situations without even realizing it.

You can transition from a growth mindset to a fixed mindset in the blink of an eye, such as when you're confronted with a specific project, a specific challenge, or an interaction with a specific person that you're not quite ready for. In these types of situations, a fixed mindset will inhibit you from learning and developing in important areas, ultimately limiting your long-term potential, too.

Everyone has various areas in their jobs where they have a more fixed mindset than a growth mindset. You might have a mental block about using a new piece of technology, having told yourself that you won't ever be able to master it.

Perhaps your role might be demanding you to take a more data-driven approach to certain tasks. And you are feeling overwhelmed by it and not quite finding the motivation or the inclination to start it.

Mindsets are often hard to change, and they often change slowly. It's easier to change our perspective than to change our thinking. – An attitude is an instant reaction formed based on how you think. It is an established accepted idea that someone or something is that specific. – A mindset is the collection of beliefs and thoughts that shape how a person thinks or processes information. These experiences impact how people make sense of the world (and self).

Stereotypes have a short-term impact. That is why they are easy to modify. Our everyday beliefs are deeply ingrained within us. They are resistant to change.

Your mindset causes your beliefs, impressions, and interpretations. It shapes the world and your relationship with yourself. Select your attitude wisely. You can create positive experiences rather than letting them be negative.

Developing a positive mindset is vital. It helps you to identify the different strategies required to complete the task. Individuals with a success mindset always seem to figure out how to make things happen in any situation, even when they seem to be impossible. Successful people tend to have difficult upbringings, but they went on to make the best of themselves. We've seen leaders battle through the toughest of times and achieve much success. Similar to each other, they all have the same commonality, a thought process or belief system called the success mindset.

A growth mindset is the one that makes you take challenges as opportunities to learn and improve. Having a rigid mindset means assuming that there are aspects of your personality or skill set that cannot be improved. A growth mindset believes that through hard work, it's possible to raise intelligence or knowledge. However, those with a fixed mindset are resistant to change in regards to their intellect. Even when you are bad at geometry, practice won't help you understand the concepts that you find difficult.

To have a positive attitude, you need to believe in your possibilities for success. It is a realistic view but does not mean you should not try. Even though your height is 5'5", if you think you can dunk, that doesn't mean that you can't - given the right training and practice. If you can realize how far you have improved your jumping shot and improve it further, you can become an even better jumper. This is the belief that positive changes can occur when we take the necessary steps to initiate change.

It takes practice to adopt a success mindset, but it also helps if you already have one. If you are confident you can change your outlook, start by taking note of your actions and observing what you can do to be more positive.

In the sales department of almost every company in every industry – these steps can start with goal setting or salesmanship. To maintain an effective learning experience, you may adapt your scripts, follow up more, or work on your listening. Whatever it is, you must have the confidence to improve and a commitment to improving.

The fact is that these situations will only get more prevalent with time. Never before has the world of work been bombed with so much change, change from all angles, change that means that businesses and the people that work within them must adapt, test, learn and challenge themselves daily.

For most, this means working hard and being willing to try new stuff. It means a shift from working in a set sphere where we know we can perform well to a sphere where there's no perceived risk of failure, of appearing incompetent. A move towards communicating with different departments and external partners and suppliers at more frequent intervals, and with people we perceive as less knowledgeable, we perceive as being more of a threat.

To be successful in today's world of work and the future, we must all learn how to flourish in challenging situations and not let our narratives control us. We must increase our persistence in dealing with challenging situations by not giving up in the end. We must look to people of the past we would have once shunned to learn from them. Essentially, we must all shift our mindset to see the world and everything in it as a never-ending opportunity to learn. When we do this, we will assure future needs to improve further as a person, an organization, or even a society.

Chapter 8 –

Take the plunge

Have you ever found yourself in a situation where you have to make a quick decision? A time during which you are extremely undecided – so much that you postpone choosing for a long time, feeling that you cannot make a choice.

Everything you encounter in life is like an opportunity. Dismissing them without positively exploring it useless, and this approach is similar to looking at an opportunity and expecting to get a positive and favorable result out of them. There is an enormous amount of value in everything, even things that we don't like. It's your job to seek out the hidden opportunities and convert those opportunities to your benefit.

Your life is driven by an unconscious mechanism and far richer than you can imagine the opportunities concealed in every step of the journey. Your role is to work through and clarify the sparks in your life trajectory.

When an opportunity arises, one must be prepared to handle and react accordingly. You must keep your eyes out for great opportunities to take advantage of them.

Ask yourself: Do you seek opportunities in your current job or business? Are you taking advantage of opportunities that arise?

Reflect on those times when you did something new outside your comfort zone and felt successful.

Ask yourself: What opportunities have you actively pursued that you feel have been beneficial?

As discussed in the last chapter, the growth mindset encourages you to believe that learning is a crucial part of life. When you are not 100 percent confident about something but still proceed with the option, it's a rewarding experience.

Ask yourself: What lessons have you learned from your career choices? What areas are you hoping to improve in your career further?

When you pursue things all the time, you develop an eye for opportunities. You get focused on planning what you want and finding ways to get it.

Ask yourself: What are the specific criteria which you use to select opportunities you are interested in? What did you discover about yourself?

You should remind yourself that your actions are bigger than you and that your actions will forever be your legacy. There are a variety of life lessons you might like to impart to the next generation. Do not wait for things to happen to you; take that first step. There's a saying, "The first step is mandatory." – that sums up everything we have discussed above. Grab the opportunities that arise in your life to improve and become the better version of yourself.

Ask yourself: In what ways would you like to be remembered? What legacy will you be leaving for future generations?

You must have heard of the statistics that only 8% of all people who set New Year's goals commit to it – that's eight people out of 100, rest 92 give up just because they are not entirely aware of the ultimate benefit of committing to their goals. Commitment makes the difference between success and failure, and it can also hurt our self-esteem if people find out that we can't be trusted. This trail further pushes us to make excuses and pointing fingers at others, distracting us from the goal.

Some people mean well when they commit but fall short primarily because of ignorance – which destroys ideas and results. In "**The British Himalayan Expedition**," W. M. Murray wrote, "*Until one is committed, there is hesitancy, the chance to draw back, always ineffectiveness. Concerning all acts of initiative and creation, there is one elementary truth, the ignorance of which kills countless ideas and splendid plans: that the moment one commits oneself, providence moves too. All sorts of things occur to help one that would never otherwise have occurred. A whole stream of events issue from the decision, raising in one's favor all manner of unforeseen incidents and meetings and material assistance, which no man could have dreamed would come his way.*"

Thoroughly plan before you go into action; a deliberate and conscious plan is required before you act. Once you have decided to do something, there is no turning back. Consider how many hours of work and how much time you have to give when committing. Specificity is the name of the game. Commit to your goals and search for new horizons. Eighty percent of the time, researchers Locke and Latham found that specific and challenging goals lead to improved performance.

You have the power to change your life with the decisions you make. When you commit to decide and take action, your life will go through radical transformations in the shortest period.

Life is just the consequence of what you've done differently from other people who have done the same thing. However, your actions have had different effects on your friends, neighbors, loved ones, relatives, etc. To set yourself on the right path, then actions must be taken.

Once you've made a decision, your life will be altered. You can change instantly if you decide to do so. The next time you feel anxious or overwhelmed, change it into an action plan instead of just sitting there doing nothing.

How is one stay interested in something and committed to it? How many times do we hear people say they want a new car, make more money, or pursue their dreams? You may make goals, but deep inside, you have not yet agreed to achieve them.

"There is a possibility I could improve, but I have no idea how." It is just fear talking, is it not? The fear that you aren't capable of doing it correctly. You have neglected to research all possible outcomes and don't have planned for all possible scenarios. This fear will keep you from deciding for the rest of your life – and you will never get off the ground. Most people overlook that all you need to do is keep the overall direction of your life open to positivity – no matter what you want to do, you will find a solution.

Decisions are difficult to make but hard to keep. Understand your goals and make your intentions clear. If you know what is most important to you, you will choose quickly and change your mind. Comparing those who aren't successful with those who are - they take a long time to make decisions and rarely change their minds.

You can change your life if you decide to be dedicated; when you stop taking "no" for an answer; when you decide to accept only one outcome; when you only agree to be focused on one conclusion – an action.

Choosing one true course of action means making sure all others are eliminated. When you decide, you are committing the result, and you have committed to achieving it. Unsuccessful people tend to make decisions based on their current predicament, while successful people decide where they want to be.

Repeating a task trains proficiency. To make sound decisions, we must make more decisions and act decisively, accept the results, and change course if necessary. The more you practice it, the better you will get at it. When you have improved your decision-making abilities, you are motivated to take your life to the next level.

Decisions have the potential to impact your relationships, your career, your health, and your emotions. This ability can tell whether you're reacting to your surroundings or making your own decisions. It can help you determine whether you are either excited or miserable. Making more decisions improves your comfort level and control over life. Deal with the cards up ahead of time. Deciding something reduces stress often - you'll be surprised at how full of energy you'll feel.

It is important to know what results you're aiming for and who you want to become. Your values and beliefs guide your behavior for both yourself as well as for others. It helps to have minimum standards so that you don't revert to your old ways. As a rule, you must raise your standards and adhere to them. Regardless of any personal hardships or tragedies, you will weather the storm.

The most important thing about decision-making power is that you already have it. Decision-making power doesn't belong to a particular group. It is up to you to summon the courage to use it. Is today your day of liberation? Would you follow your dreams today?

Look forward to decisions, because every decision will affect your life in some way. It is entirely possible that what you do next, what you read, where you go next, who you listen to, or where you stand during checkout will trigger an idea for you. Life is full of unexpected twists and turns. If you want to live it to the fullest, then you must be prepared to take control and ready to seize every opportunity that presents itself to you.

Chapter 9 –

Play the winning game

Many people's understanding of personal finances is on the level that money comes in and goes out. Calculating some numbers can assist you in assessing your current financial status and guiding your long-term financial objectives.

It is critical to establish your net worth, calculated as your net assets minus your liabilities. And debts (what you owe). Then, subtract your debts from your assets to get your net worth.

Your net worth describes where you are at that moment, and it is perfectly natural for it to change over time. Updating your net worth is helpful because you will regularly learn real value (at least quarterly). Tracking your net worth over time gives you a clearer view of your progress, identifies what you've accomplished, and highlights areas you need to work on.

When there is more money available, the majority of people will spend more. As individuals move into the senior levels of their careers, there tends to be a corresponding increase in "lifestyle inflation." Though you might pay your bills, lifestyle inflation can hurt you in the long run. Every dollar you spend is less in the future and during retirement.

It's not uncommon for friends and coworkers to mimic each other's habits. When you go on vacations with your peers, they might expect you to travel in first class, stay at exclusive resorts, and dine in expensive restaurants. The Adams (who are spending heavily in your circle) have accumulated decades of debt to keep their upscale image. Though the material benefits were abundant – expensive cars, frequent vacations, and private school for the children – the Adams might still be unable to save a single cent for retirement.

As your professional and personal income grows, some expenditures are appropriate. You may need to upgrade your wardrobe to accommodate a larger family, or you might have to buy a larger house. It might make sense to get a lawnmower service, freeing up time for family and socializing while also improving your quality of life.

It is in your best interest to know the difference between "needs" and "desires" to make better budgeting decisions. Needs are the items required to live: food, shelter, healthcare, and transportation. Desires are things you would like to have but don't require.

It can be difficult to differentiate between needs and desires. To work and to take the kids to school, you require a vehicle. You prefer the nicer car that costs twice as much as a normal car (and costs you more in gas). There are no doubts about the existence of a "need," but that doesn't make it a "desire." The price difference between an economy car and a luxury car is the money you didn't have to spend.

Your needs must get top billing in your budget. As soon as your needs have been met, you should begin to save money for discretionary items. Also, if you have any money remaining at the end of each week or each month after covering your real necessities – save it.

Most people believe that money expands one's options, but it cannot replace contentment. Inner peace is something that gives you a reliable and lasting sense of well-being.

If you dread leaving your Job because you don't like it, then your mental and physical health can be adversely affected in the long term. In 2014, research showed that employees had rated income fourth in their list of factors that influence their level of job satisfaction, behind the ability to balance work and nonwork demands, work itself, and job security. There are other benefits. If you are content with your career path, you will be more likely to work hard with a sense of purpose, thus increasing your chances of finding fulfillment.

When we think of the future, we are free to follow our dreams, but there are reasons why we cannot attain these goals in the near or long term. There are good reasons to stay in your current job, like "staying and providing for the kids" or "facing the risk of losing the regular flow of income," or "retirement planning and savings," plus there is the constant fear of never being able to "have the money."

Most of our lives we will spend working, so we might as well do something we are truly passionate about and let the time pass us by. Bronnie Ware mentions in her book 'The Top Five Regrets of the Dying' that the top regret of those who are dying is not having the courage to follow their heart. Time is the most valuable resource. Go for your dreams while you are young, while you are physically fit, because there will be no regrets about what you might have done later.

Work-life will never be easy; there will always be stress in your environment. Happiness will help you persist through the bad days at work.

Employers look for forward-looking, active, and prepared employees who can be resourceful with information and support. A happy person is more likely to be a candidate for advancement than working and constantly strained. Besides, when you reach the pinnacle of your work, you will be satisfied with knowing that you have found your true purpose.

It's possible to pursue your passion even if you don't know where it will lead. Nothing can be achieved without risk. It can be a good time to discover your real interests and talents if you feel unfulfilled in your career. You may not be able to immediately transition into a new career due to financial issues, familial obligations, or a need to upskill. Invest in saving to make your goal a possibility rather than trying to pursue a long-term goal.

Learning from all the amazingly wealthy and successful people is true for each of them that those people followed their heart with logical and conscious decisions rather than following a road blindly. Even when they made money their priority – they did it systematically and logically. They knew what they wanted to do and how they are going to achieve it. They understood the value of their time and their life – and that's what kept them motivated and kept them on track for success and having all the wealth and experience they got.

For someone reading about them and learning their ways, keep in mind that it is extremely vital to capitalize on the resources you have in-hand because that's the only way to move forwards. Your resources include your time, assets, personal and professional connections – you must learn to use them to carve yourself a successful career path – or help you build a billion-dollar business.

Whatever you think is your calling, and whatever is it that you decide to choose for yourself, make sure that you are happy with it. Make sure that it helps you get out of bed with motivation and focus. And after working on it for three, four, or five decades, you won't get tired of it. Ensure that whatever you decide to do, it helps you with internal peace and satisfaction because if you are not peaceful inside, no matter how much money you have in the bank, it won't let you be satisfied with your life.

We are here on this planet for a limited time, and there's only one chance to live right. We can spend it making money with poor health and less value of life, or we can spend it making money with good health and high value of life – both are achievable depending on how you play the game.

Your financial status, age, or ethnicity does not matter because hard work can elevate you towards your goals and help you achieve goals – the only demand is your dedication and belief in yourself and your goals.

Some people started their journey from nothing and now employ thousands of people to help them achieve heights many of us can't even imagine. Those people are not extraordinary, and they aren't blessed with unnatural abilities or skills. The only difference they have is that they don't understand the word 'failure,' they don't understand the meaning of 'giving up, they are stubborn when it comes to achieving excellence, they are investors who dare to invest in their dreams without looking at financial statements, ledgers and future financial projections.

Be You – believe in yourself, trust your journey - walk, run, crawl but never… never give up. Keep going.

Made in the USA
Monee, IL
04 November 2026

67385783R00046